50 Premium Chili Dishes

By: Kelly Johnson

Table of Contents

- Classic Texas Brisket Chili
- Wagyu Beef and Black Bean Chili
- Smoky Chipotle Short Rib Chili
- White Chicken and Hatch Chile Chili
- Spicy Venison and Chorizo Chili
- Lobster and Corn Chowder Chili
- Bison and Fire-Roasted Tomato Chili
- Smoked Duck and Bourbon Chili
- Thai Red Curry Coconut Chili
- Pulled Pork and Pineapple Chili
- Lamb and Moroccan Spice Chili
- Korean Bulgogi and Kimchi Chili
- Green Chili with Tomatillo and Pork
- Brazilian Feijoada-Inspired Chili
- Italian Sausage and White Bean Chili
- Blue Crab and Andouille Chili
- Beef and Mole Poblano Chili
- Cocoa-Infused Espresso Chili
- Buffalo Chicken and Blue Cheese Chili
- Wild Boar and Sweet Potato Chili
- Shrimp and Jalapeño Cornbread Chili
- Chimichurri Flank Steak Chili
- Roasted Poblano and Black Bean Chili
- Ghost Pepper and Smoked Turkey Chili
- Beer-Braised Oxtail Chili
- Maple Bacon and Bourbon Chili
- Filet Mignon and Roasted Garlic Chili
- Persian Lamb and Pomegranate Chili
- Szechuan Peppercorn and Five-Spice Chili
- Spicy Vegan Jackfruit Chili
- Coconut-Lime Chicken Chili
- Smoked Salmon and Dill Chili
- Chipotle Pumpkin and Black Bean Chili
- Cherrywood Smoked Brisket Chili
- Italian Porcini Mushroom Chili

- Truffle Oil and Parmesan White Bean Chili
- Korean Gochujang Pork Belly Chili
- Caribbean Jerk Chicken and Mango Chili
- Lobster Bisque and Saffron Chili
- Guinness Stout and Ground Sirloin Chili
- Honey Glazed Duck and Orange Chili
- Chipotle Chocolate and Cinnamon Chili
- Roasted Red Pepper and Eggplant Chili
- Argentine Chimichurri Beef Chili
- Smoked Sausage and Lentil Chili
- Almond Butter and Thai Basil Chili
- French Cassoulet-Style Chili
- Cajun Alligator and Creole Spice Chili
- Miso and Shiitake Mushroom Chili
- Pecan-Smoked Pork Shoulder Chili

Classic Texas Brisket Chili

Ingredients:

- 2 lbs smoked brisket, chopped
- 2 tbsp vegetable oil
- 1 large onion, diced
- 4 cloves garlic, minced
- 2 tbsp chili powder
- 1 tbsp smoked paprika
- 1 tbsp ground cumin
- 1 tsp cayenne pepper
- 1 tsp oregano
- 1 tsp salt
- 1/2 tsp black pepper
- 1 can (14.5 oz) diced tomatoes
- 1 can (6 oz) tomato paste
- 2 cups beef broth
- 1 can (15 oz) kidney beans, drained (optional)
- 1 can (15 oz) pinto beans, drained (optional)

Instructions:

1. Heat vegetable oil in a large pot over medium heat. Add onion and garlic, sauté until softened.
2. Stir in chili powder, paprika, cumin, cayenne, oregano, salt, and black pepper. Cook for 1 minute.
3. Add chopped brisket and cook for 5 minutes, stirring occasionally.
4. Pour in diced tomatoes, tomato paste, and beef broth. Bring to a simmer.
5. Reduce heat to low and let simmer for 45 minutes, stirring occasionally.
6. If using beans, add them in the last 15 minutes of cooking.
7. Adjust seasoning to taste and serve hot.

Wagyu Beef and Black Bean Chili

Ingredients:

- 2 lbs Wagyu beef, cubed
- 2 tbsp olive oil
- 1 onion, diced
- 4 cloves garlic, minced
- 1 tbsp chili powder
- 1 tsp smoked paprika
- 1 tsp ground cumin
- 1/2 tsp cayenne pepper
- 1 can (14.5 oz) diced tomatoes
- 1 can (15 oz) black beans, drained
- 2 cups beef broth
- Salt and pepper to taste

Instructions:

1. Heat olive oil in a large pot over medium heat. Add onion and garlic, sauté until softened.
2. Add Wagyu beef, browning on all sides.
3. Stir in chili powder, paprika, cumin, cayenne, salt, and pepper.
4. Add diced tomatoes, black beans, and beef broth. Bring to a simmer.
5. Reduce heat and cook for 1 hour, stirring occasionally.

Smoky Chipotle Short Rib Chili

Ingredients:

- 2 lbs short ribs, bone-in
- 2 tbsp vegetable oil
- 1 onion, diced
- 3 cloves garlic, minced
- 2 chipotle peppers in adobo sauce, chopped
- 1 tbsp smoked paprika
- 1 tsp cumin
- 1 tsp oregano
- 1 can (14.5 oz) crushed tomatoes
- 2 cups beef broth
- Salt and pepper to taste

Instructions:

1. Heat oil in a pot, sear short ribs on all sides. Remove and set aside.
2. Sauté onion and garlic, then add chipotle peppers, paprika, cumin, and oregano.
3. Return short ribs to pot, add tomatoes and broth. Bring to a boil.
4. Reduce heat, cover, and simmer for 2.5 hours until meat is tender.

White Chicken and Hatch Chile Chili

Ingredients:

- 2 lbs chicken breast, shredded
- 2 tbsp olive oil
- 1 onion, diced
- 4 cloves garlic, minced
- 2 roasted Hatch chiles, chopped
- 1 can (15 oz) white beans, drained
- 4 cups chicken broth
- 1 tsp cumin
- 1/2 tsp coriander
- 1/2 tsp salt

Instructions:

1. Sauté onion and garlic in olive oil. Add Hatch chiles and spices.
2. Stir in chicken, white beans, and broth.
3. Simmer for 30 minutes, stirring occasionally.

Spicy Venison and Chorizo Chili

Ingredients:

- 1 lb ground venison
- 1/2 lb chorizo, crumbled
- 1 onion, diced
- 3 cloves garlic, minced
- 1 tbsp chili powder
- 1 tsp cayenne pepper
- 1 can (14.5 oz) diced tomatoes
- 1 can (15 oz) kidney beans, drained
- 2 cups beef broth

Instructions:

1. Brown venison and chorizo in a pot. Remove excess fat.
2. Add onion, garlic, and spices. Sauté until fragrant.
3. Stir in tomatoes, beans, and broth. Simmer for 45 minutes.

Lobster and Corn Chowder Chili

Ingredients:

- 2 lobster tails, chopped
- 2 tbsp butter
- 1 onion, diced
- 2 cloves garlic, minced
- 1 cup corn kernels
- 2 cups seafood stock
- 1/2 cup heavy cream
- 1 tsp smoked paprika

Instructions:

1. Sauté onion and garlic in butter. Add corn and paprika.
2. Pour in seafood stock, bring to a simmer.
3. Add lobster and cream, cook for 10 minutes.

Bison and Fire-Roasted Tomato Chili

Ingredients:

- 1 lb ground bison
- 1 tbsp olive oil
- 1 onion, diced
- 3 cloves garlic, minced
- 1 can (14.5 oz) fire-roasted tomatoes
- 2 cups beef broth
- 1 tsp cumin
- 1/2 tsp smoked paprika

Instructions:

1. Sauté onion and garlic in olive oil.
2. Add bison, cook until browned.
3. Stir in tomatoes, broth, and spices. Simmer for 1 hour.

Smoked Duck and Bourbon Chili

Ingredients:

- 2 smoked duck breasts, diced
- 1 tbsp olive oil
- 1 onion, diced
- 3 cloves garlic, minced
- 1/4 cup bourbon
- 1 can (14.5 oz) diced tomatoes
- 2 cups chicken broth
- 1 tsp smoked paprika

Instructions:

1. Sauté onion and garlic in olive oil.
2. Add duck and bourbon, cook for 5 minutes.
3. Stir in tomatoes, broth, and spices. Simmer for 45 minutes.

Thai Red Curry Coconut Chili

Ingredients:

- 1 lb ground chicken
- 2 tbsp red curry paste
- 1 can (14 oz) coconut milk
- 1 red bell pepper, sliced
- 2 cups chicken broth
- 1 tsp fish sauce

Instructions:

1. Brown chicken in a pot. Stir in curry paste.
2. Add coconut milk, broth, bell pepper, and fish sauce. Simmer for 30 minutes.

Pulled Pork and Pineapple Chili

Ingredients:

- 2 lbs pulled pork
- 1 tbsp olive oil
- 1 onion, diced
- 2 cloves garlic, minced
- 1 cup pineapple chunks
- 1 can (14.5 oz) diced tomatoes
- 2 cups chicken broth

Instructions:

1. Sauté onion and garlic in olive oil.
2. Add pulled pork, pineapple, tomatoes, and broth.
3. Simmer for 45 minutes.

Lamb and Moroccan Spice Chili

Ingredients:

- 1 lb ground lamb
- 1 tbsp olive oil
- 1 onion, diced
- 3 cloves garlic, minced
- 1 tsp cinnamon
- 1 tsp cumin
- 1 can (14.5 oz) diced tomatoes
- 2 cups beef broth

Instructions:

1. Sauté onion and garlic in olive oil.
2. Brown lamb, then stir in spices.
3. Add tomatoes and broth, simmer for 1 hour.

Korean Bulgogi and Kimchi Chili

Ingredients:

- 1 lb bulgogi beef
- 1 cup kimchi, chopped
- 1 tbsp sesame oil
- 1 onion, diced
- 2 cloves garlic, minced
- 2 cups beef broth
- 1 tsp gochujang

Instructions:

1. Sauté onion and garlic in sesame oil.
2. Add bulgogi beef, cook until browned.
3. Stir in kimchi, gochujang, and broth. Simmer for 30 minutes.

Green Chili with Tomatillo and Pork

Ingredients:

- 2 lbs pork shoulder, cubed
- 1 tbsp olive oil
- 1 onion, diced
- 4 cloves garlic, minced
- 6 tomatillos, husked and chopped
- 2 roasted poblano peppers, diced
- 2 cups chicken broth
- 1 tsp cumin
- 1/2 tsp oregano
- Salt and pepper to taste

Instructions:

1. Heat oil in a pot, brown pork.
2. Add onion, garlic, tomatillos, and peppers, sauté for 5 minutes.
3. Stir in broth and spices, simmer for 1.5 hours.

Brazilian Feijoada-Inspired Chili

Ingredients:

- 1 lb pork belly, diced
- 1 lb smoked sausage, sliced
- 1 onion, diced
- 4 cloves garlic, minced
- 1 can (15 oz) black beans, drained
- 1 can (14.5 oz) diced tomatoes
- 2 cups beef broth
- 1 tsp smoked paprika

Instructions:

1. Brown pork belly and sausage in a pot.
2. Add onion, garlic, and paprika, cook for 3 minutes.
3. Stir in beans, tomatoes, and broth, simmer for 1 hour.

Italian Sausage and White Bean Chili

Ingredients:

- 1 lb Italian sausage, crumbled
- 1 tbsp olive oil
- 1 onion, diced
- 3 cloves garlic, minced
- 1 can (15 oz) white beans, drained
- 1 can (14.5 oz) diced tomatoes
- 2 cups chicken broth
- 1 tsp fennel seeds

Instructions:

1. Heat oil, brown sausage.
2. Add onion, garlic, and fennel seeds, cook for 5 minutes.
3. Stir in beans, tomatoes, and broth, simmer for 45 minutes.

Blue Crab and Andouille Chili

Ingredients:

- 1 lb lump blue crab meat
- 1/2 lb Andouille sausage, diced
- 1 tbsp butter
- 1 onion, diced
- 2 cloves garlic, minced
- 1 can (14.5 oz) diced tomatoes
- 2 cups seafood stock
- 1/2 cup heavy cream

Instructions:

1. Sauté sausage, onion, and garlic in butter.
2. Stir in tomatoes and seafood stock, simmer for 30 minutes.
3. Add crab and cream, cook for 10 minutes.

Beef and Mole Poblano Chili

Ingredients:

- 2 lbs beef chuck, cubed
- 1 tbsp vegetable oil
- 1 onion, diced
- 4 cloves garlic, minced
- 2 dried ancho chiles, rehydrated and blended
- 1 oz dark chocolate
- 1 tsp cinnamon
- 1 tsp cumin
- 2 cups beef broth

Instructions:

1. Brown beef in oil.
2. Add onion, garlic, and blended ancho chiles, cook for 5 minutes.
3. Stir in chocolate, cinnamon, cumin, and broth, simmer for 2 hours.

Cocoa-Infused Espresso Chili

Ingredients:

- 1 lb ground beef
- 1 tbsp olive oil
- 1 onion, diced
- 3 cloves garlic, minced
- 1 tbsp cocoa powder
- 1/2 cup brewed espresso
- 1 can (14.5 oz) diced tomatoes
- 2 cups beef broth

Instructions:

1. Sauté onion and garlic in oil.
2. Brown beef, then stir in cocoa powder and espresso.
3. Add tomatoes and broth, simmer for 1 hour.

Buffalo Chicken and Blue Cheese Chili

Ingredients:

- 2 lbs shredded chicken
- 1 tbsp butter
- 1 onion, diced
- 3 cloves garlic, minced
- 1/2 cup buffalo sauce
- 1 can (14.5 oz) diced tomatoes
- 2 cups chicken broth
- 1/2 cup crumbled blue cheese

Instructions:

1. Sauté onion and garlic in butter.
2. Add chicken, buffalo sauce, tomatoes, and broth. Simmer for 30 minutes.
3. Stir in blue cheese before serving.

Wild Boar and Sweet Potato Chili

Ingredients:

- 1 lb ground wild boar
- 1 tbsp olive oil
- 1 onion, diced
- 3 cloves garlic, minced
- 1 sweet potato, diced
- 1 can (14.5 oz) diced tomatoes
- 2 cups beef broth
- 1 tsp smoked paprika

Instructions:

1. Brown boar in oil.
2. Add onion, garlic, sweet potato, and paprika, cook for 5 minutes.
3. Stir in tomatoes and broth, simmer for 1 hour.

Shrimp and Jalapeño Cornbread Chili

Ingredients:

- 1 lb shrimp, peeled and deveined
- 1 tbsp butter
- 1 onion, diced
- 2 cloves garlic, minced
- 1 jalapeño, chopped
- 1 can (14.5 oz) diced tomatoes
- 2 cups seafood stock
- 1/2 cup cornmeal

Instructions:

1. Sauté onion, garlic, and jalapeño in butter.
2. Add tomatoes and seafood stock, bring to a simmer.
3. Stir in shrimp and cornmeal, cook for 10 minutes.

Chimichurri Flank Steak Chili

Ingredients:

- 1 lb flank steak, diced
- 1 tbsp olive oil
- 1 onion, diced
- 3 cloves garlic, minced
- 1 can (14.5 oz) diced tomatoes
- 2 cups beef broth
- 1/2 cup chimichurri sauce

Instructions:

1. Brown flank steak in oil.
2. Add onion, garlic, and tomatoes, cook for 5 minutes.
3. Stir in broth and simmer for 1 hour.
4. Mix in chimichurri before serving.

Roasted Poblano and Black Bean Chili

Ingredients:

- 3 roasted poblano peppers, diced
- 1 tbsp olive oil
- 1 onion, diced
- 3 cloves garlic, minced
- 1 can (15 oz) black beans, drained
- 1 can (14.5 oz) diced tomatoes
- 2 cups vegetable broth
- 1 tsp cumin
- 1/2 tsp smoked paprika

Instructions:

1. Sauté onion and garlic in olive oil.
2. Stir in poblanos, black beans, tomatoes, broth, and spices.
3. Simmer for 30 minutes, stirring occasionally.

Ghost Pepper and Smoked Turkey Chili

Ingredients:

- 2 cups smoked turkey, shredded
- 1 tbsp vegetable oil
- 1 onion, diced
- 2 cloves garlic, minced
- 1 small ghost pepper, finely minced (use gloves)
- 1 can (14.5 oz) fire-roasted tomatoes
- 2 cups chicken broth
- 1 tsp chili powder
- 1/2 tsp black pepper

Instructions:

1. Sauté onion, garlic, and ghost pepper in oil.
2. Add turkey, tomatoes, broth, and spices. Simmer for 40 minutes.

Beer-Braised Oxtail Chili

Ingredients:

- 2 lbs oxtail
- 1 tbsp olive oil
- 1 onion, diced
- 3 cloves garlic, minced
- 1 bottle dark beer
- 1 can (14.5 oz) crushed tomatoes
- 2 cups beef broth
- 1 tsp cumin
- 1/2 tsp smoked paprika

Instructions:

1. Sear oxtail in oil, remove and set aside.
2. Sauté onion and garlic, then deglaze with beer.
3. Add oxtail, tomatoes, broth, and spices. Simmer for 3 hours until tender.

Maple Bacon and Bourbon Chili

Ingredients:

- 6 slices thick-cut bacon, chopped
- 1 tbsp butter
- 1 onion, diced
- 3 cloves garlic, minced
- 1/4 cup bourbon
- 1/4 cup maple syrup
- 1 can (14.5 oz) diced tomatoes
- 2 cups beef broth

Instructions:

1. Cook bacon until crispy, remove and set aside.
2. Sauté onion and garlic in bacon fat and butter.
3. Deglaze with bourbon, then add maple syrup, tomatoes, broth, and bacon. Simmer for 45 minutes.

Filet Mignon and Roasted Garlic Chili

Ingredients:

- 1 lb filet mignon, cubed
- 1 tbsp olive oil
- 1 head garlic, roasted and mashed
- 1 onion, diced
- 1 can (14.5 oz) fire-roasted tomatoes
- 2 cups beef broth
- 1 tsp cumin
- 1/2 tsp smoked paprika

Instructions:

1. Sear filet mignon in oil, remove and set aside.
2. Sauté onion, then add roasted garlic, tomatoes, broth, and spices.
3. Return steak and simmer for 20 minutes.

Persian Lamb and Pomegranate Chili

Ingredients:

- 1 lb ground lamb
- 1 tbsp olive oil
- 1 onion, diced
- 3 cloves garlic, minced
- 1/2 cup pomegranate juice
- 1 can (14.5 oz) diced tomatoes
- 2 cups beef broth
- 1 tsp cinnamon
- 1/2 tsp ground cumin

Instructions:

1. Brown lamb in oil.
2. Sauté onion and garlic, then stir in pomegranate juice.
3. Add tomatoes, broth, and spices. Simmer for 1 hour.

Szechuan Peppercorn and Five-Spice Chili

Ingredients:

- 1 lb ground beef or pork
- 1 tbsp vegetable oil
- 1 onion, diced
- 3 cloves garlic, minced
- 1 tsp Szechuan peppercorns, crushed
- 1/2 tsp Chinese five-spice powder
- 1 can (14.5 oz) diced tomatoes
- 2 cups beef broth
- 1 tbsp soy sauce

Instructions:

1. Brown meat in oil.
2. Sauté onion, garlic, Szechuan peppercorns, and five-spice powder.
3. Add tomatoes, broth, and soy sauce. Simmer for 45 minutes.

Spicy Vegan Jackfruit Chili

Ingredients:

- 2 cups jackfruit, shredded
- 1 tbsp olive oil
- 1 onion, diced
- 3 cloves garlic, minced
- 1 can (14.5 oz) diced tomatoes
- 1 can (15 oz) kidney beans, drained
- 2 cups vegetable broth
- 1 tsp chili powder
- 1/2 tsp cayenne

Instructions:

1. Sauté onion and garlic in oil.
2. Add jackfruit, tomatoes, beans, broth, and spices. Simmer for 45 minutes.

Coconut-Lime Chicken Chili

Ingredients:

- 2 lbs shredded chicken
- 1 tbsp coconut oil
- 1 onion, diced
- 3 cloves garlic, minced
- 1 can (14 oz) coconut milk
- 2 cups chicken broth
- Juice of 1 lime
- 1 tsp curry powder

Instructions:

1. Sauté onion and garlic in coconut oil.
2. Add chicken, coconut milk, broth, lime juice, and curry powder.
3. Simmer for 30 minutes.

Smoked Salmon and Dill Chili

Ingredients:

- 1/2 lb smoked salmon, flaked
- 1 tbsp butter
- 1 onion, diced
- 2 cloves garlic, minced
- 1 can (14.5 oz) diced tomatoes
- 2 cups vegetable broth
- 1 tsp fresh dill, chopped
- 1/2 cup heavy cream

Instructions:

1. Sauté onion and garlic in butter.
2. Stir in tomatoes, broth, and dill, simmer for 20 minutes.
3. Add smoked salmon and cream, cook for 5 minutes.

Chipotle Pumpkin and Black Bean Chili

Ingredients:

- 1 can (15 oz) pumpkin puree
- 1 can (15 oz) black beans, drained
- 1 tbsp olive oil
- 1 onion, diced
- 3 cloves garlic, minced
- 1 chipotle pepper in adobo, minced
- 1 can (14.5 oz) diced tomatoes
- 2 cups vegetable broth
- 1 tsp cumin
- 1/2 tsp smoked paprika

Instructions:

1. Sauté onion and garlic in olive oil.
2. Add chipotle, black beans, pumpkin, tomatoes, broth, and spices.
3. Simmer for 30 minutes, stirring occasionally.

Cherrywood Smoked Brisket Chili

Ingredients:

- 2 lbs smoked brisket, chopped
- 1 tbsp vegetable oil
- 1 onion, diced
- 3 cloves garlic, minced
- 1 can (14.5 oz) fire-roasted tomatoes
- 2 cups beef broth
- 1 tsp chili powder
- 1/2 tsp smoked paprika

Instructions:

1. Sauté onion and garlic in oil.
2. Add brisket, tomatoes, broth, and spices. Simmer for 45 minutes.

Italian Porcini Mushroom Chili

Ingredients:

- 1 cup dried porcini mushrooms, rehydrated and chopped
- 1 lb ground beef
- 1 tbsp olive oil
- 1 onion, diced
- 3 cloves garlic, minced
- 1 can (14.5 oz) diced tomatoes
- 2 cups beef broth
- 1 tsp oregano
- 1/2 tsp red pepper flakes

Instructions:

1. Sauté onion and garlic in oil.
2. Brown beef, then stir in mushrooms, tomatoes, broth, and spices.
3. Simmer for 1 hour.

Truffle Oil and Parmesan White Bean Chili

Ingredients:

- 1 can (15 oz) white beans, drained
- 1 tbsp olive oil
- 1 onion, diced
- 3 cloves garlic, minced
- 2 cups vegetable broth
- 1/2 cup grated Parmesan cheese
- 1 tbsp white truffle oil

Instructions:

1. Sauté onion and garlic in olive oil.
2. Add beans and broth, simmer for 30 minutes.
3. Stir in Parmesan and drizzle with truffle oil before serving.

Korean Gochujang Pork Belly Chili

Ingredients:

- 1 lb pork belly, cubed
- 1 tbsp sesame oil
- 1 onion, diced
- 3 cloves garlic, minced
- 2 tbsp gochujang (Korean chili paste)
- 1 can (14.5 oz) diced tomatoes
- 2 cups beef broth
- 1 tsp soy sauce

Instructions:

1. Sauté pork belly in sesame oil until crispy.
2. Add onion, garlic, gochujang, and soy sauce.
3. Stir in tomatoes and broth, simmer for 45 minutes.

Caribbean Jerk Chicken and Mango Chili

Ingredients:

- 2 lbs shredded jerk chicken
- 1 tbsp coconut oil
- 1 onion, diced
- 3 cloves garlic, minced
- 1 cup diced mango
- 1 can (14.5 oz) diced tomatoes
- 2 cups chicken broth

Instructions:

1. Sauté onion and garlic in coconut oil.
2. Add jerk chicken, mango, tomatoes, and broth. Simmer for 30 minutes.

Lobster Bisque and Saffron Chili

Ingredients:

- 2 lobster tails, chopped
- 1 tbsp butter
- 1 onion, diced
- 2 cloves garlic, minced
- 1 pinch saffron
- 2 cups seafood stock
- 1/2 cup heavy cream

Instructions:

1. Sauté onion and garlic in butter.
2. Stir in saffron, seafood stock, and heavy cream.
3. Add lobster and simmer for 10 minutes.

Guinness Stout and Ground Sirloin Chili

Ingredients:

- 1 lb ground sirloin
- 1 tbsp olive oil
- 1 onion, diced
- 3 cloves garlic, minced
- 1 can (14.5 oz) diced tomatoes
- 1 bottle Guinness stout
- 2 cups beef broth
- 1 tsp Worcestershire sauce

Instructions:

1. Brown sirloin in oil.
2. Add onion, garlic, tomatoes, Guinness, broth, and Worcestershire.
3. Simmer for 1 hour.

Honey Glazed Duck and Orange Chili

Ingredients:

- 2 duck breasts, diced
- 1 tbsp honey
- 1 tbsp olive oil
- 1 onion, diced
- 2 cloves garlic, minced
- Juice of 1 orange
- 1 can (14.5 oz) diced tomatoes
- 2 cups chicken broth

Instructions:

1. Glaze duck with honey and sear in oil.
2. Sauté onion and garlic, then add duck, orange juice, tomatoes, and broth.
3. Simmer for 45 minutes.

Chipotle Chocolate and Cinnamon Chili

Ingredients:

- 1 lb ground beef
- 1 tbsp olive oil
- 1 onion, diced
- 3 cloves garlic, minced
- 1 tbsp cocoa powder
- 1 chipotle pepper in adobo, minced
- 1/2 tsp cinnamon
- 1 can (14.5 oz) diced tomatoes
- 2 cups beef broth

Instructions:

1. Brown beef in oil.
2. Sauté onion, garlic, and chipotle.
3. Stir in cocoa powder, cinnamon, tomatoes, and broth. Simmer for 1 hour.

Roasted Red Pepper and Eggplant Chili

Ingredients:

- 2 red bell peppers, roasted, peeled, and diced
- 1 medium eggplant, diced
- 1 tbsp olive oil
- 1 onion, diced
- 3 cloves garlic, minced
- 1 can (14.5 oz) diced tomatoes
- 2 cups vegetable broth
- 1 tsp smoked paprika
- 1/2 tsp cumin

Instructions:

1. Sauté onion and garlic in olive oil.
2. Add eggplant and cook until softened.
3. Stir in roasted red peppers, tomatoes, broth, and spices.
4. Simmer for 30 minutes, stirring occasionally.

Argentine Chimichurri Beef Chili

Ingredients:

- 1 lb beef chuck, cubed
- 1 tbsp olive oil
- 1 onion, diced
- 3 cloves garlic, minced
- 1 can (14.5 oz) diced tomatoes
- 2 cups beef broth
- 1/2 cup chimichurri sauce

Instructions:

1. Sear beef in oil, remove and set aside.
2. Sauté onion and garlic, then add tomatoes and broth.
3. Return beef to pot and simmer for 1.5 hours.
4. Stir in chimichurri before serving.

Smoked Sausage and Lentil Chili

Ingredients:

- 1 lb smoked sausage, sliced
- 1 tbsp olive oil
- 1 onion, diced
- 2 cloves garlic, minced
- 1 cup lentils, rinsed
- 1 can (14.5 oz) diced tomatoes
- 2 cups chicken broth
- 1/2 tsp thyme

Instructions:

1. Sauté onion and garlic in olive oil.
2. Add sausage, lentils, tomatoes, broth, and thyme.
3. Simmer for 45 minutes until lentils are tender.

Almond Butter and Thai Basil Chili

Ingredients:

- 1 lb ground turkey or chicken
- 1 tbsp coconut oil
- 1 onion, diced
- 3 cloves garlic, minced
- 1/4 cup almond butter
- 1 can (14.5 oz) diced tomatoes
- 2 cups chicken broth
- 1 tbsp soy sauce
- 1/2 cup Thai basil, chopped

Instructions:

1. Brown turkey in coconut oil.
2. Add onion, garlic, and almond butter, stir until combined.
3. Stir in tomatoes, broth, and soy sauce. Simmer for 40 minutes.
4. Stir in Thai basil before serving.

French Cassoulet-Style Chili

Ingredients:

- 1/2 lb duck confit, shredded
- 1/2 lb pork sausage, sliced
- 1 can (15 oz) white beans, drained
- 1 tbsp olive oil
- 1 onion, diced
- 3 cloves garlic, minced
- 1 can (14.5 oz) diced tomatoes
- 2 cups chicken broth
- 1/2 tsp thyme

Instructions:

1. Sauté onion and garlic in olive oil.
2. Add duck confit, sausage, beans, tomatoes, broth, and thyme.
3. Simmer for 45 minutes.

Cajun Alligator and Creole Spice Chili

Ingredients:

- 1 lb alligator meat, cubed
- 1 tbsp vegetable oil
- 1 onion, diced
- 3 cloves garlic, minced
- 1 tbsp Creole seasoning
- 1 can (14.5 oz) diced tomatoes
- 2 cups chicken broth

Instructions:

1. Brown alligator meat in oil.
2. Add onion, garlic, and Creole seasoning, cook for 5 minutes.
3. Stir in tomatoes and broth, simmer for 45 minutes.

Miso and Shiitake Mushroom Chili

Ingredients:

- 1 cup shiitake mushrooms, sliced
- 1 tbsp sesame oil
- 1 onion, diced
- 3 cloves garlic, minced
- 1 tbsp white miso paste
- 1 can (14.5 oz) diced tomatoes
- 2 cups vegetable broth

Instructions:

1. Sauté onion, garlic, and mushrooms in sesame oil.
2. Stir in miso paste, tomatoes, and broth.
3. Simmer for 30 minutes.

Pecan-Smoked Pork Shoulder Chili

Ingredients:

- 2 lbs pecan-smoked pork shoulder, shredded
- 1 tbsp vegetable oil
- 1 onion, diced
- 3 cloves garlic, minced
- 1 can (14.5 oz) diced tomatoes
- 2 cups chicken broth
- 1 tsp smoked paprika

Instructions:

1. Sauté onion and garlic in oil.
2. Stir in pork, tomatoes, broth, and paprika.
3. Simmer for 45 minutes.

www.ingramcontent.com/pod-product-compliance
Lightning Source LLC
LaVergne TN
LVHW081459060526
838201LV00056BA/2832